MAPLE FLAG

Mike Reyno

CONCORD
PUBLICATIONS COMPANY

We welcome authors who can help
expand our range of books. If you
would like to submit material, please
feel free to contact us.

We are always on the look-out for new,
unpublished photos for this series.
If you have photos or slides or
information you feel may be useful to
future volumes, please send them to us
for possible future publication.
Full photo credits will be given upon
publication.

ISBN 962-361-032-7
Printed in Hong Kong

FRONT COVER

Armed with four AIM-9's F-15E displays the overall sleek lines. The F-15E has kept all its air-to-air qualities that are found on the F-15C. In this picture you can also see that the refueling receptacle is opened to take on fuel. For Maple Flag missions air-to-air refueling was not necessary, this picture was taken on the way to "Fighter Town Canada" from Seymour Johnson. (Photo by Jeff Wilson)

BACK COVER

A top view of a CF-18 shows the overall shape of Canada's premier fighter.

All photos by Mike Reyno unless otherwise stated.

Maple Flag emerged from discussions held in 1977 when the commander of Tactical Air Command (TAC) the United States Air Force (USAF) at that time, Gen. bert Dixon and the commander of Canadian Air Command, LGen. Bill Carr, discussed the need of for exercise similar to Red Flag held at Nellis AFB, evada, to be held in Canada. Restrictions at Nellis ere beginning to interfere with the training at Red g. At this time Canada had no real experience in nning Flag exercise's so both countries agreed that d Flag staff from Nellis would run Maple Flag until the nadians felt confident enough to run the exercise emselves. CFB Cold Lake, Alberta, often referred to "Fighter Town Canada" located 300km north-west Edmonton was chosen as the location for Maple g as it already has a massive range to support such exercise.

CFB Cold Lake and the Cold Lake Air Weapons nge (CLAWR) was considered the best location for aple Flag for several reasons; freedom from air traffic straints, the sparse population in the area, and cause the topography was similar to European nditions. The rolling terrain, lakes and similar nditions were a far cry from those found flying over e desert in Nevada. Training was improved over Red g because pilot's were flying in conditions and over rain which would be found in Central Europe which as considered to be where hostilities would erupt at at time.

The weapons range at CFB Cold Lake is over 3,000 uare miles in size for ordinance, and 7,000 square les of exercise area, similar in size to Kuwait. The size the range allows for varied route selection for the gress/egress and also permits air-to-air engagements th minimal restrictions, those restrictions often being e squadron standard operational procedures. The nge itself contains over seventy tactical target mplexes including airfields, truck parks, tanks, idges, convoys, AAA and SAM sites. All targets are nstructed at 2/3 scale, and usually found in small earings making them difficult to acquire and attack, erefore giving the pilot's better training in acquiring rgets at low level and at a high speed.

The VFR conditions at Cold Lake allow for rapid unches and recoveries, and avoid the training which ay be lost at Nellis AFB due to the many flight strictions. The lack of IFR constraints allowed the troduction of a higher intensity level of realism by lowing mass radio silent air launches, as well as mock tacks on CFB Cold Lake itself.

In 1978, when the first Maple Flag was held, it was n by the people of Red Flag from Nellis AFB, with anadian officers watching in the background to oserve how the exercise was to be run. The mericans ran the exercise until 1981 at which time anada took over. Up until 1987 Maple Flag was run -annually, it is now run annually to give the quadron's based at Cold Lake more time to

concentrate on their own training. Each Maple Flag is six weeks long and divided into three periods to give different squadrons from Canada, England and the U.S. an opportunity to participate in Maple Flag.

A large portion of support and funding for Maple Flag comes from the U.S.A.F. which brings threat emitters from Nellis AFB, Nevada. The threat emitters give a realistic simulation of flying over "enemy" territory making Maple Flag more realistic. Aircraft support equipment and personnel from Red Flag also come to Cold Lake to provide any assistance when needed, however Maple Flag is totally Canadian run.

Maj. Bill Motriuk, organizer and operations officer for Maple Flag XXV, and a well seasoned fighter pilot, has brought Canadian, British and American air forces together to fight, in the words of Maj. Motriuk, "a generic threat, but a highly sophisticated threat." The theme or scenario of Maple Flag XXV had changed from previous exercises. In past Maple Flag's the emphasize has been placed on a central European conflict theme. With 1 Canadian Air Group ceasing air operations in Germany by December 31, 1992, the war in central Europe seems highly unlikely with the break-up of the Soviet Union and the WARSAW PACT. Since the Gulf War took place in 1991, events have changed the theme of Maple Flag XXV. The emphasize has changed from a high-intensity type scenario to a medium intensity conflict. Instead of superpowers battling over Central Europe, it seems more likely that NATO countries would be called upon to enforce U.N. sanctions against a particular country which is militarily well equipped, such as Iraq was.

Maple Flag XXV was the first Flag exercise to change its theme to a medium-intensity type conflict with a non-WARSAW PACT nation. Lessons from the Gulf War were embedded into Maple Flag, as well as new ideas which were not used in the Gulf War were practiced. "The Maple Flag XXV threat has a better trained and more well equipped air force then that of the Iraqis. " states a press release from CFB Cold Lake. This allows participants at Maple Flag to fight a more challenging and aggressive force.

Red Flag personnel from Nellis AFB in Nevada were also in abundance to offer any assistance to Maple Flag staff. The main assets from Red Flag are those of the 57th FWW which supplied six F-16C aggressor aircraft to simulate a hostile enemy. The 57th FWW can simulate the tactics of most "hostile nations" which primarily fly MiG aircraft. The 57th has brought its knowledge to assist in providing a more realistic threat at Maple Flag. LCol. Sams, assistant director of operations for Red Flag , stated, "Since we do Red Flag more often than the Canadians do Maple Flag, we're up here to offer any assistance we can to the Maple Flag staff, but it is a Canadian show and we are very impressed with how the exercise has developed and what it has been able to offer. We also like the idea of how there are very few restrictions compared to a Red

Flag."

The purpose behind a Maple Flag exercise is not to see who can beat who, but to learn the tactics of an opposing or defending force in a real scenario, such as what happened in the Persian Gulf. Different squadrons come to Maple Flag to acquire fighter tactics and how to effectively operate in large strike packages. Most of the junior air crews at Maple Flag XXV have never flown in large strike packages comprising of 77 or more aircraft. The crews have six weeks to develop their skills. They take back what they have learned at Maple Flag to their respective squadron's and share this new knowledge.

Maple Flag exercises have given Canadian, British and American fighter and attack pilots the opportunity to work closely with each other with no one coun dominating the planning of strikes on the range. Ea air arm has also been able to see how each oth operates and come up with new and better metho of how to operate. In the long run, Maple Fl exercises save lives in real combat situations. If some these crews did not have the experience of goi through Flag exercises here in Canada or in the Unit States, many crews may have lost their lives in t Persian Gulf. Maj. Motriuk summed it up best, "Pilo are taught valuable lessons here at Maple Flag a they'll never forget what they have been taught he because if they were "killed" here on the range th they would have been killed in a real situation, th learn by their mistakes."

MAPLE FLAG XXV PARTICIPANTS

	UNIT	PLACE	TYPE	NUMBER	PERIOD
U.S.A.F.	388th TFW	Hill AFB	F-16C	10	All
	31st TFW	Homestead AFB	F-16C	6	All
	69th TFS	Moody AFB	F-16C	6	PD.3
	33rd TFW	Eglin AFB	F-15C	10	All
	27th TFW	Cannon AFB	F-111D	6	All
	57th FWW	Nellis AFB	F-16C	6	All
	155th TRG	Lincoln N.B.	RF-4C	6	PD.1
	4th TFW	Seymour Johnson AFB	F-15E	6	PD.2
	67th TRW	Bergstrom AFB	RF-4C	6	PD.2,3
	138th TFG	Tulsa, O.K.	A-7D	6	PD.2
	908th TAG	Maxwell AFB	C-130E	2	PD.3
	910th TAG	Youngstown Municiple Airport, Ohio	C-130E	2	PD.3
	911th TAG	Greater Pittsburg Int. Airport	C-130E	2	PD.3
	914th TAG	Dobbins AFB	C-130E	2	PD.3
	165th TAG	Savanah, Georgia	C-130E	2	PD.1
	552nd AWACW	Tinker AFB	E-3B	1	All
	37th ARS	Fort Warren, Wy.	UH-1N	3	All
C.A.F.	433 TFS	CFB Bagotville	CF-18A	4	PD.2
	410 TFTS	CFB Cold Lake	CF-18A/B	8	PD.2,3
	416 TFS	CFB Cold Lake	CF-18A/B	12	All
	441 TFS	CFB Cold Lake	CF-18A	4	PD.1
	425 TFS	CFB Bagotville	CF-18A/B	8	All
	ATG	CFB Namao	CC-130E	2/launch	PD.3
	119 AD BTY	CFB Chatham			
	42 RDR	CFB Cold Lake			
R.A.F.	* 6 Sqn.	RAF Coltishall	Jaguar	9	All
	41 Sqn.				
	54 Sqn.				

*6,41 and 54 Sqn. shared nine Jaguars with each Squadron rotating each period

Period Dates	Period 1 - 25 April - 9 May 1992
	Period 2 - 9 May - 23 May 1992
	Period 3 - 23 May - 6 June 1992

CFB COLD LAKE

In the late 1940's Canada was running out of locations to operate aircraft which were testing weapons systems. Most other RCAF bases at that time were unsuitable because they were located near populated areas. In 1951 it was announced that a site had been found where weapons could be dropped or fired and jet aircraft could operate without restrictions other than those at the squadron level. The site was found on the Alberta-Saskatchewan border some 300km north west of Edmonton. The weapons range was 33 miles deep by 104 miles long. In 1954 RACF Station Cold Lake was opened for operations.

The first unit at Cold Lake was the Air Armament Evaluation Detachment (AAED) of the Central Experimental and Proving Establishment. Today the unit is called AETE (Aerospace Engineering Test Establishment) and maintains a fleet of 18 aircraft. Cold Lake was home to CF-100 Canucks and T-33 Silverstars when they were in their prime in the 50's. Cold Lake became Canada's "Fighter Town" and would see every fighter that has ever been in Canada's inventory be based at Cold Lake. In 1968 RCAF Station Cold Lake became CFB Cold Lake with the unification of the Armed Forces. CF-104 Starfighter's, CF-101 Voodoo's and CF-5 Freedom Fighter's would be screaming over the un-populated areas daily with crews being permitted to fly supersonic down to 100 feet and sometimes pilots ventured lower.

In 1982 CFB Cold Lake received Canada's pride and joy from St. Louis Missouri, the CF-18 Hornet. 410 "Cougars" TFTS was the first unit to receive the CF-18 and is responsible for all aircrew training on the Hornet. Today 416 "Lynx" TFS and 441 "Silver Fox" TFS are also CF-18 users other than 410 TFTS. Other units which reside at the base also include 419 "Moose" TFTS which flies the CF-5 Freedom Fighter, AETE, which flies a mixed fleet of aircraft and Base Flight which flies CT-133 Silver Stars and CH-118 Iroquois.

CFB Cold Lake, "Fighter Town Canada" or "Cool Lake", which ever name you choose has become known as one of the modern fighter bases in NATO. Today the total size of the range besides the weapons delivery range is approximately the size of the country of Kuwait. Cold Lake has proven to be an ideal location for Maple Flag and NATO exercise's as well for the very limited restrictions and the absence of civilian air traffic. Cold Lake has been able to provide the crews with enough realism to fight a battle on its ranges which resemble the terrain found in central Europe where it was once thought to be the location of hostilities. The base handles over some 145,000 aircraft movements per year. With three large runways it is no wonder Cold Lake can handle the amount of traffic it does. Cold Lake has a population of approximately 3,200 military personnel as well as another 3,340 dependents.

Special thanks must go to the following people. Without their assistance this book would not have been made possible.

Capt. Tony White, CAF
Capt. Jane Thompson, CAF
Maj. Bill Motriuk, CAF
Capt. Darren Cockell, CAF
SGT. Donald Clapham, CAF
SGT. David Gariepy, CAF
W.O. Randy Steed, CAF
S/L Graham Wright, RAF
OCDT. Greg Bend, CAF
David F. Brown
Jeff Wilson
Larry Milberry
Mike Valenti
Robbie Shaw
Duncan MacIntosh
Tony Cassanova
Andy Cline
Heather Cleveland

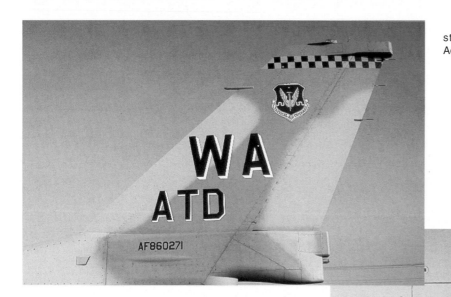

The tail of an F-16 from the 57th FWW. The "WA" tail code stands for Weapons Analysis and the "ATD" stands for Adversary Tactics Division.

The 57th FWW came from Nellis AFB to participate in Maple Flag XXV to act as aggressor's against the opposing forces. As of June 1, 1992 the 57th FWW will become known as the 57th FW under ACC (Air Combat Command).

Once known as the 64th AS until October 1990, the unit deactivated due to budget restraints and became known as the Adversary Tactics Division of the 4440th TFTG, better known as Red Flag which operates a fleet of 8 F-16C's, 6 of which they brought to Maple Flag.

An F-16C (86-0271) painted in the "Fulcrum" paint scheme represents the MiG-29. Note the Russian style two digit numbers on the intake.

This F-16C (87-0267) is being manned by LCol. Sams, assistant director of Red Flag at Nellis AFB. LCol. Sams was at Maple Flag to assist staff in planning and as you can see here, to play a little with the opposing force.

With speed brakes open, F-16C (86-0251) returns from the range after playing with CF-18's, F-16's and F-15's. This view also shows how big the Pratt & Whitney F100-PW-220 engines are. Although not as powerful as the General Electric F110, the USAF decided to go with the F100 for its fleet of Aggressor's because of its dependability.

The 57th FWW operates block 32 F-16C's. Here 86-0269 returns with 86-0272 back to the apron. Notice the SUU-20 practice pod on the center line weapons station. Each launch at Maple Flag would see four F-16's of the 57th participate with two more serving as back up.

A "Flogger" painted F-16 (87-0269) awaits its pilot for the morning launch.

The 57th FWW was usually one of the first units to launch for each mission. The 57th brought its wealth of knowledge to Maple Flag to pass onto Canadian, British and American crews participating.

The 421st "Black Widows" FS, a TAC unit subordinate to the 388th TFW from Hill AFB. The 421st was a TFS and with the restructuring became known as FS as of June 1st. The wing will also come under the direction of the 12th Air Force under ACC.

The commanding officer's aircraft, 88-0421, is from the 40th production block which sees all F-16's AMRAAM capable. The aircraft carries inert Sidewinders on the wing tip rails and 25lbs. practice bombs on the inboard pylon. The 421st FS flew in the attack role during Maple Flag as part of the opposing force.

88-0432 ready for the next launch. The 421st was part of the 388th TFW (Provisional) during Desert Storm and flew out of Alminhad, United Arab Emirates. The 421st was primarily tasked with air-to-ground sorties.

Maple Flag can be hard on pilots, aircraft and ground crew alike. TSGT Steve Little changes a tire on an F-16.

Two F-16's prepare to launch on 30R for the morning mission. The 421st FS brought 10 F-16's to CFB Cold Lake for Maple Flag XXV. Each launch would see eight F-16's from the 421st on the schedule. The runways are long enough at Cold Lake that it is not necessary for aircraft to launch in afterburner if they so desire.

With canopies raised and aircraft loaded with fuel and practice ordinance, a line of 421st F-16's readies for an early morning mission.

88-0432 returns after a successful morning strike against the defending Fantasians. This was all too familiar to the 421st FS which participated in Desert Storm from January 1991 until March the same year. The 421st brought its hard lessons learned from the Persian Gulf War to Maple Flag.

The 309th FS, 31st FW from Homestead AFB sent six F-16C's to participate in Maple Flag XXV to fly air-to-ground strikes. The fighting "Donald Duck" denotes this squadron as the "Wild Ducks". The 309th was formed at Ft. Wayne, Indiana in 1942 equipped with the P-40. The 309th has flown 10 different types of aircraft up to the F-16C. In 1944 the 309th had the credit of destroying 30 German aircraft in a single mission.

89-2134 armed with inert AIM-9's returns from a morning hop. The 309th would launch four aircraft each mission.

Capt. Vanrooyen returns from a successful afternoon hop. He looks rather cool in the 80 degree heat at Cold Lake.

F-16 90-0710 taxi's to its holding place before the morning launch. With integration the 309th FS, 31st FW will come under the command of the 9th Air Force. 1992 saw the units first visit to Maple Flag.

The 27th TFW brought the F-111D Aardvark to Maple Flag for the last time. The 27th originated from 27th Bombardment Group (Light), activated on Feb.1, 1940, at Barksdale AFB. Since that time the 27th has operated 3 different aircraft types and now resides at Cannon AFB, New Mexico.

The 522nd TFS was responsible for the six F-111D's which participated in Maple Flag.

F-111D's are in the process of being re-painted in an overall gunship grey scheme which is also found on the F-15E Strike Eagle. This one is returning from a strike mission over the CLAWR. Four F-111's would take part in each launch.

F-111D's share the line with F-15C's at Maple Flag. "Switchblades" are carrying SUU-20 pods and AIM-9 Sidewinders.

One can appreciate the power that resides in these beasts. The F-111D is equipped with the Pratt and Whitney TF-30-P-9 engine which can generate 20,840lbs of static thrust.

A victim carrying two SUU-20's
[an]d one AIM-9, an F-111 returns from
[a] strike package. A GR.MK.1 Jaguar of
[No]. 6 Sqn. scored a simulated kill on
[it]s prey. In the background is an F-
[5]C from the 57th FWW.

With flaps down and spoilers extended F-111D 68-0169 heads to the active while a brother F-111 goes to afterburner. Although wearing a low viz
[na]tional insignia, the "Fireballs" were able to keep a high viz squadron patch and 27th TFW patch on the nose.

A close-up of an SUU-20 on an F-
[11]1 armed with six 25lb. practice
[b]ombs. Each F-111 would carry two
[p]ods and one AIM-9 Sidewinder.

In full afterburner F-111 68-0157 starts to roll to join three other F-111's just launched. He will return overhead within 50 minutes with empty pods.

Lt. Barnes displays a "thumbs up" after returning from the afternoon strike package. Although the aircraft wears a high viz 27th TFW patch it al carries a low viz 27th FW patch which will be under ACC. The 27th FW will come under the command of the 8th Air Force.

With wings extended and wing gloves fully deployed, two "Switch Blades" taxi to the active. One can learn to appreciate the overall size of the F-11 The 27th participated in periods one and two of Maple Flag.

Awaiting their time to taxi for the afternoon launch, crew chiefs wait for the departure time. 68-0178 will taxi out only to abort due to a hydraulic problem. In the background are CT-133 Silver Stars which belong to Cold Lake Base Flight. They are used for air taxi's, to tow targets and simulate inbound missiles.

CF-18 188786 sits in the evening sun. This CF-18 just came in from CFB Bagotville to participate in Maple Flag, hence the fuel tanks. This aircraft belongs to 433 "Porcupine" TFS.

188777 of 441 "Silver Fox" TFS awaits its pilot. Notice the six bomb missions below the LEX. Canada had participated in the Persian Gulf War flyi͏ air operations out of Quatar. Under "Operation Friction" Canada committed 26 CF-18's to the coalition force and came up with the name "Desert Cats" ͏ CF-18's based in the Gulf because all three squadrons which were used has a type of cat as their symbol.

416 "Lynx" TFS had six CF-18's participating in Maple Flag. 416 is based at CFB Cold Lake so providing the aircraft was not difficult. Here a CF-18͏ (188938) returns to its home. Notice on the wing fence, below Canada, is written "Check Six" in Arabic. The aircraft is also carrying an ACMI on the wing t͏ rail.

425 "Alouttes" TFS from CFB Bagotville, P.Q. brought 10 CF-18's to Maple Flag. 425 was responsible for flying escort missions during the exercise. It is unusual to see the last three numbers not painted in the nose of the aircraft. This CF-18 is 188915.

Crews work on CF-18A 188767 of 441 TFS. This aircraft was recently received from the now defunct 409 "Nighthawk" TFS which was deactivated upon returning from the Gulf. 409 was based out of CFB Baden Sollingen. As of December 31, 1992 all air operations will cease to operate at Baden as Defence cuts have also hit Canada with the closing of two bases in Germany. CF-18's will now only be located at CFB Cold Lake and CFB Bagotville.

With flaps lowered a CF-18B returns from an escort mission. Notice how the back seat is empty. Canada had acquired 138 CF-18's of which 27 were duals, with the majority serving with 410 "Cougars" TFTS at Cold Lake.

Armament crews load the M61A1 Vulcan, 20-mm rotary cannon on a 410 CF-18B.

410 Sqn. is the training squadron for all CF-18 pilots. This aircraft is ready to head to the CLAWR with a full load of ammunition and fuel.

Six CF-18's from 433 "Porqupine" TFS came to Cold Lake to fight it out with the best. 188788 is carrying two 330 US gal. fuel tanks. The official designation of Canada's "electric jet" is CF-188 but is commonly known as the CF-18. Hornet is also not officially adopted because it is not bilingual to French.

Carrying one SUU-20 on the right wing, a CF-18 displays the false canopy which is painted on the underside of the fighter, this will give pilots that extra few seconds to gain the advantage in a fight. The USN and USMC are beginning to do the same thing to their fleet of F/A-18's. (Canadian Forces via Author)

Going ballistic, a CF-18A of 410 TFTS reaches for the sky. With a thrust to weight ratio of 2-to-1 the CF-18 can climb with ease. (Canadian Forces via Author)

Two ground crew members top up 188929 with JP-4. Notice the Cougar on the wing fence, meaning this aircraft belongs to 410 Sqn.

Maj. Jim Donihee of 441 Sqn. listens to the briefing given by Maple Flag and Red Flag staff. Maj. Donihee was commander of the four plane strike package for the morning launch.

close up of a Canadian SUU-20.

88787 of 433 returns after 50 minutes of seat of the pants flying.

A fighter pilot's dream, CF-18's as far as the eye can see. "Fighter Town Canada" is home to three CF-18 units with each squadron maintaining a fleet of 16 aircraft.

Bombs, bombs and more bombs. Cement filled MK.82's lie on the grass in front of 410's hanger. 410 loads up CF-18's with the cement filled bombs for target practice and to enable pilots to acquire the different handling found when carrying the ordinance.

Four CF-18's crawl down the taxi way heading for the active. In th[is] view you can also appreciate how rugged the landing gear really is.

A CF-18B of 416 Sqn. heads f[or] the ramp. The CF-18B has the sam[e] capabilities as the A model but cann[ot] carry as much fuel.

188780 of 416 "Lynx" TFS heads for 30R. This aircraft carries two bomb mission's painted on the side of the aircraft, vestiges of its Gulf War participation.

A CF-18 (188725) of 425 TFS returns from a morning hop. This day saw eight CF-18's of 425 launch to defend against the opposing force.

Capt. "KCAACK" Cockell of 441 "Silver Fox" TFS mounts up in 188781. This is his second mission of the day.

A CF-18A (188783) of 433 "Porqupine" TFS taxi's in from an afternoon hop. Notice how the "Canadian Forces" which is usually on both sides of the roundle has been placed back by the tail.

A CF-18 of 433 TFS is chained down for tests of its GE F404-GE-400 low bypass turbo fan engines. The only convenient time to do this was in the late evening when everything isn't so hectic. This makes the workload on ground crew that much more difficult. (Photo by Robbie Shaw via Author)

The 173rd TRS, 155th TRG brought tears to the eye with the unit being only one of a handful left flying the Phantom. The 173rd TRS brought six RF-4C to Maple Flag. This RF-4C, 65-0923, was recently received from the 190th TRS/124th TRG, Idaho ANG. In 1994 a sad end will come to the 173rd TRS when they will exchange their RF-4C's for KC-135's.

Nose art, "Hawg Wild" displayed on 65-0824.

You dirty waskel! "Elmer" displayed on 65-0828.

"Betty Boop" holds the American Flag on 65-0859. It would be nice if other units were able to adopt the same type of nose art.

Baking in the afternoon sun, 65-0917, is being readied for the next morning's launch. Note the intake screen installed on the right intake while the ground crew were performing engine run-ups.

TSGT Ted Turkington and SSGT Thimgan change the Photographic Flare Dispenser, used for photo flashes, this is located on both sides of the aircraft.

Sharing the ramp with F-16C's of the 388th TFW, RF-4C's of the 173rd prepare to mount up for engine start and taxi for takeoff.

With engines at full throttle, two F-4's launch into the morning sun. The 173rd would send four aircraft on each mission. At this pace some crews were flying twice a day.

65-0824 is the last to return with results from the morning assault on the Fantasians. The 173rd will show the impact of the opposing forces' might. The RF-4C is 4 ft. 8 ins longer than the F-4C to accommodate the different radar suite and camera's.

With Maj. Ouellette at the controls and Capt. Evans in the back seat, "Elmer", heads for the active. The reconnaissance version of the F-4 dates back to 1963 of which 503 were produced.

RF-4C 66-0428 is the first of four Phantoms launched from the 173rd TRS. Note the knife painted on the splinter plate.

66-0428 is the second Phantom to wear "Rambo" nose art. The first was 65-0878. The second was appropriate named "Rambo II".

The 60th FS, the "Fighting Crows". is part of the 33rd FW from Eglin AFB, Florida. The "Fighting Crows" had just changed their unit badge from the 60th TFS to the 60th FS for Maple Flag XXV. You may recognize the crow with the Tommy gun as Heckle or Jeckle. Both the 59th and 60th FS provided pilot's for Desert Storm to the 58th FS which also belongs to the 33rd FW.

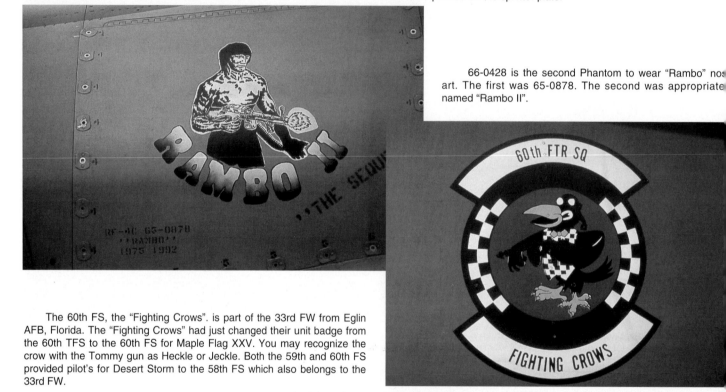

An RF-4C Phantom, 67-0450, belonging to the 67th TRW arrives from Bergstrom AFB carrying three external fuel tanks for the long journey from Texas to Alberta. Like the 173rd, the 67th would launch four RF-4's on each mission.

F-15C 85-0118 is a very distinctive Eagle within the 33rd. This F-15 belongs to the Wing Commander, Col. Greg Martin. Besides the shadowed EG and 33 FW, the tail also contains the squadron colours of the 58th, 59th and 60th FS's. 37 Iraqi aircraft were downed by F-15C Eagles during the Gulf War.

Col. Greg Martin's personal mount "Gulf Spirit" is one of many F-15's which have worn the distinctive personal markings of the 33rd.

The badges of the squadrons within the 33rd FW.

A close-up of the tail markings of "Gulf Spirit".

How much more lowviz can you get? F-15C 85-0095 displays the new camouflage scheme which will adorn all F-15's in the near future, Pacific Grey. At least the squadron crest has stayed in the high viz colours. Under the wing is a CT-133 and a CT-114 Tutor which both belong to AETE.

Not only has the colour scheme changed they have also changed the Eagle emblem on the insides of the tail. Now the Eagle looks more sleek and fierce.

Considered the supreme in the art of air-to-air combat, (you may have to argue with a CF-18 pilot about that) the F-16 has been an excellent choice as an aggressor aircraft for the USAF and the USN. The USAF, unlike the USN, has retained the M61A1 20mm cannon and the capability to carry weapons.

Ground crew ready 86-0269 for a Maple Flag launch. F-16's of the 57th were acting as part of the defending force against the large strike packages.

88-0452 is having minor adjustments made after a Maple Flag launch as a CF-5A(R) Freedom Fighter of 419 TFTS taxis out for a training mission. The 421st shared 419's ramp along with RAF Jaguars and RF-4C Phantoms.

A FOD screen sits in front of a [...]
16. The FOD screen enables t[...]
crews to perform engine run-u[...]
without ingesting debris or son[...]
unlucky fellow.

Two F-16C's of the 421st return from another low level bombing mission. Aircrew from the 421st commented favorably on the absence of so mar[...] restrictions which are in place at Red Flag.

The 309th operates the newest version of the "Viper", F-16C's - block 50. The commanding officer takes 90-0709 to the end of runway 30R while tw[...] CF-18's prepare to launch.

F-111D 68-0088 heads for the active. All F-111's were armed with
UU-20 pods and practice AIM-9 Sidewinders. The F-111D along with the
newly configured F-111G will have been retired by the time this book
reaches print. They will be replaced by the F-111E and F-111F.

CF-18A 188725 returns from
escorting strike packages to their
target. This CF-18 belongs to 425 Sqn.
from CFB Bagotville, P.Q. The patch
on the tail which is covered over is that
of 439 Sqn. from CFB Baden
Sollingen.

CF-18A 188798 of 416 was one of
two CF-18's which scored a ship kill
during the Gulf War. USN A-6 Intruders
had expended of all their ordinance on
the target and called on two CF-18's
which were in the area. After several
passes and expending of all their
ammunition from the gun, the pilot
locked on with an AIM-7 Sparrow and
scored a kill, hence the ship with the X
through it. 188915 is also the last CF-
18A built.

A CF-18B of 410 "Cougar" TFTS,
188933 flies over the CLAWR carrying
two SUU-27 pods. 410 provided eight
CF-18's for Maple Flag. The CF-18
was first used in Maple Flag back in
1984. (Canadian Forces via Author)

Holding at the end of 30R, fou
CF-18's of 416 TFS head out for
morning hop. If this was an America
base this would be the last chanc
where all arming pins are pulled, a
Canadian bases this is all done befo
the aircraft leaves the apron.

Although this aircraft wears the
markings of 409 "Nighthawk" TFS, this
aircraft actually belongs to 416. 409
was disbanded after the Persian Gulf
War with aircraft being allocated to
other squadrons. This CF-18 is
returning to Cold Lake after DACM with
F-16's of the 57th FWW. (Photo by
Robbie Shaw via Author)

With a ground crewman
performing any last checks, RF-4C 65-
0838, "D.I. Joe" is hooked up to the
APU for start up. CF-18's and F-16's
make their way to the active with the
RF-4 following shortly behind.

The 173rd was the last unit to launch and the last to recover during Maple Flag. Phantoms were sent in at low level with CF-18 escorts to photograph the damage. All RF-4's were also carrying a 600-US gal fuel tank on the centerline.

Home based at Bergstorm AFB, Texas, the 12th TRS, 67th TRW also brought six RF-4's. The 12th TRS participated during periods 2 and 3 replacing the 173rd. (Dave Brown via Author)

F-15C 85-0121 displays the 60th TFS on the tail. Armed with a practice AIM-9 Sidewinder the Eagle makes the long journey down to the end of the runway. The Eagles of the 33rd would rotate with CF-18 Hornets of 425 TFS to fly escort on the opposing force or fly with the defending force, the bad guys.

F-15C 86-0169 is towed out for start up at the 1992 London International Air Show. 16 F-15's took part in "A Gathering of Eagles". This Eagle will finally makes its way home after several weeks away from home. But the London Air Show was a great stop over.

Two F-15E's from the 336th FS the "Rocketeers". The 336th fle hundreds of missions during Dese Storm, the crews were able to brir the knowledge acquired during th Persian Gulf War to Maple Flag. Som crew remarked that Maple Flag was some ways more difficult, although th bullets are not real at Maple Fla (Photo by David F. Brown)

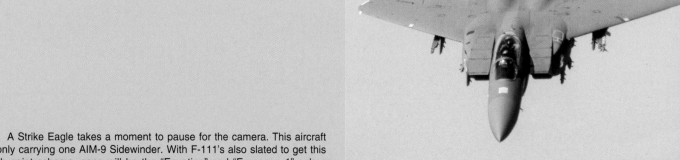

A Strike Eagle takes a moment to pause for the camera. This aircraft is only carrying one AIM-9 Sidewinder. With F-111's also slated to get this drab paint scheme, gone will be the "Egyptian" and "European 1" colour schemes which adorn many fighters in the inventory. (Photo by David F. Brown)

419 "Moose" TFTS is responsible for all training of fighter pilots moving on to the CF-18. 419 maintains a fleet of over 30 CF-5A/D Freedom Fighters and can train up to 24 students every six months. 419 is also tasked for aggressor support to various bases in Canada and the U.S. They have participated in numerous Maple Flag exercises over the past years but was overburdened this year to participate in this years event.

To celebrate the receiving of the colours and the 50th anniversary of the squadron, the "Moosemen" decorated CF-5A 116740 in the squadron colours.

In 1991 410 "Cougar" TFTS celebrated its 50th anniversary in a special way by painting CF-18A 188749 in the "Cougars" colours, complete with red false canopy on the underside. Unfortunately this paint scheme did not last very long. 410 maintains a fleet of 27 CF-18A/B's with most of them being duals. (Photo by Canadian Forces)

Two CC-130E's of 426 Sqn. from CFB Trenton prepare to head for the deck with incoming defensive air from the defending forces. CF-18's are ready to fight off the attackers and make sure the Hercules is able to perform its task to resupply the troops. (Photo by Larry Milberry)

A ground crewman closes up a GR.MK.1A Jaguar of N 54 Sqn. with an impending storm coming on. (Photo by Mi Valenti)

This superb photo can make anyone appreciate the 101. The Voodo served a proud history in Canada's air arm serving as an alert aircraft fo many years for NORAD. The last Voodoo was retired from Canadia service in 1987 at CFB North Bay, Ont. The Voodoo flew escort durin previous Flag exercises. (Photo by Robbie Shaw)

XX733 taxi's out for an afternoon strike. RAF Jaguars were one of the last to launch to add that final blow to the defending forces. This Jaguar was flown by S/L Bagshaw during the Persian Gulf War. His brother is Canadian Lt. Col. Bagshaw, commanding officer of 421 TFS flying CF-18's out of CFB Baden Sollingen, Germany.

S/L Davis is being helped to strap into his machine. Jaguar crews ar not used to flying the Jaguar like it should be in the U.K. due to low leve restrictions. The Jaguar fit right in on the CLAWR in being able to fly lo level strikes against the defending force.

With intake covers having just been removed, two F-15's are readied for a morning launch with the canopies opened to reduce the heat in the cockpit. The 33rd brought 10 F-15's to Maple Flag with each of the three squadrons within the 33rd rotating every two weeks.

Two F-15C's launch in afterburner armed with AIM-9's to the CLAWR. All aircraft are able to fly supersonic on the range down to an altitude of 100 feet. The Eagles will return after 50 minutes of "yanking and banking" with CF-18's of 425 TFS and F-16's of the 57th FWW.

85-0097 bakes in the afternoon sun. The warm weather followed the Eagles from Florida with average temperatures at Cold Lake 26 degrees Celsius and above, not bad when you consider that the base is located 300km north east of Edmonton. In the background is a CH-136 Kiowa hovering about to make its way to the range to pick up operators working on the threat emitters.

An F-15 from the 58th FS takes off in afterburner to escort the opposing force, the good guys. The 33rd operated the MSIP F-15C which houses the APG-70 radar which was originally only slated for the F-15E Strike Eagle. (Photo by Larry Milberry)

With the "barn door" opening an Eagle returns from an afternoon mission. This F-15 "downed" two of the defending forces CF-18's and F-16's.

An F-15C of the 60th TFS begins the long trek to the end of 30R.

The 59th FS also participated at Maple Flag XXV which enabled all three squadrons within the 33rd FW to participate.

An F-15C takes off in full afterburner at Cold Lake in the hazy sky. The climbing rate of the F-15 will put anyone at ease.

Two F-15C of the 59th TFS had just come from Maple Flag XXV to participate in the 1992 Molson Canadian London International Air Show, a Gathering of Eagles". The 59th had sent 10 F-15C's to Maple Flag.

KC-10A Extender's were used to ferry in equipment for Maple Flag. C-141's, C-130's and C-5's were also used.

The 4th Wing came with six F-15E Strike Eagles from Seymour Johnson AFB, North Carolina. The 4th was the first wing to be redesignated from a TFW when KC-10A Extender's were put under it's command and now under the command of ACC. In 1988 the 4th began to replace its fleet of F-4E Phantoms with the F-15E. (Photo by Jeff Wilson)

Three Strike Eagles fly formation off of a KC-10. The F-15E has given the 4th a jump ahead in technology since replacing the F-4E. The Strike Eagle proved to be a valuable weapons system during Desert Storm. (Photo by Jeff Wilson)

SSGT Odom polishes up the windscreen before greeting the crew for the afternoon launch. The 4th would launch four Strike Eagles on each mission with some crews flying twice a day. (Photo by Jeff Wilson)

Two ground crew work on an engine problem on 90-0231 to have the aircraft ready for the afternoon strike package. Maple Flag staff commented that was nice to see TAC's newest aircraft able to participate in the exercise. This gave Canadian and British crews the chance to work in close quarters with the Strike Eagle. (Photo by Mike Valenti)

Probably about the most colour you will ever see on a Strike Eagle is with the intake wraps still on. On this day the morning launch was canceled due to the low ceiling, remarkable considering everything was done at low level. (Photo by Mike Valenti)

Armed with an AIM-9 and also carrying a LANTIRN pod, an F-15E heads skyward, behind will follow three more Strikes. On this mission CF-18's, F-16's F-111's and Jaguar's were flying air-to-ground missions. CF-18's and F-16's were also flying escort. (Photo by Larry Milberry)

Carrying a LANTIRN pod a Strike Eagle, 90-0231, takes off in afterburner. The morning launch was canceled due to the poor weather, however it cleared enough for the afternoon launch. (Photo by Mike Valenti)

Four Strike Eagles return from an afternoon strike against the Fantasians. The Eagles proved to be successful on this mission. Unlike other exercises the U.S. such as William Tell and Gun Smoke, Maple Flag does not keep "scores" of units participating in the exercise. People are here to learn and train with the best, not to see who's better. (Photo by Mike Valenti)

A crew chief helps an Eagle Driver and his WSO strap into their machine as a CF-18A carrying a SUU-20 and an ACMI taxi's back to its nest. (Photo by Larry Milberry)

F-15E (90-1706) lands after arriving from Seymour Johnson. Note the travel pods.

Staff at Cold Lake have done a fine job in displaying this CF-5A Freedom Fighter (116736) from 419 TFTS complete with a dummy pilot at the bases main gate.

This aerial view shows how big Cold Lake really is. With eight hangers all fighter aircraft can be kept indoors so needed, especially during the cold winter. On the far left is where 419 is located with its own ramp to itself.

You wouldn't have to guess twice about who's territory you are in. 410 [i]s also responsible for running a Fighter Weapons Instructor Course which [i]s the Canadian version of "Top Gun".

The Silver Fox Den is home to 441 TFTS, the "Silver Fox" Sqn.

441 Sqn. was also celebrating its 50th anniversary in the [C]anadian Forces. 441 was unable to decorate its aircraft as [e]laborate as 410, however they were able to add some colour [t]o the tail with the black and white checker board which is [u]sually drab grey and the 50th anniversary patch.

Cold Lake is also home to 416 "Lynx" TFS, 188793 displays two bomb mission symbols that were claimed during the Persian Gulf War. 416 was the [l]ast squadron in the Canadian Forces to fly the CF-101 Voodoo. Unfortunately lost with the Voodoo were the colourful markings of that time, now its drab or [d]rabier.

AETE is the biggest user of the weapons delivery range at Cold Lake, the Primrose Lake Range. Here a CF-18A is firing the Canadian made CRV-rockets that are made by Bristol Aerospace. AETE maintains three CF-18's including one dual. (Photo by AETE)

A CF-5A holds at the end of 30R. The red X easily identifies this aircraft as the property of AETE. The white strip down the fuselage is for photographing weapons delivery. This CF-5, 116702, is the second CF-5 off of the production line and the oldest CF-5 in the Canadian Forces.

Another unit based at Cold Lake that is often over looked is Base Flight which maintains a fleet of 10 CT-133's and three CH-118 Iroquois. Pictured here is a CH-118, 118103, this is one of ten still in Canadian service.

Carrying two DELMAR targets a CT-133 flies profiles for CF-18's and CF-5's. The DELMAR targets can be reeled out 2 miles behind the aircraft for target practice. Besides working for the fighters, the T-bird is also used as an air taxi for people and much needed parts. T-birds have also on occasion mixed it up with CF-18's, F-16's and F-15's and in the hands of a well seasoned fighter pilot, have scored "kills" against their much younger and potent cousins.

This close up of a topographic map shows how big the range is at Cold Lake, housing over 70 tactical targets. (Photo by Canadian Forces)

Forming a vital link in the chain at Cold Lake is the base fire dept. which can be seen roaring around the ramps at Cold Lake during Maple Flag. crew takes time out after a Maple Flag recovery to pose for the camera. From left to right are; Sgt. Donald Clapham, Col. Norm Hollis and Cpl. Joh Hardacre, RAF.

Cpl. Leo Roy gives clearance for the first group to retur from a strike mission. The air traffic controllers had their hand full with each launch and recovery during the exercise.

Also able to practice their skills at Maple Flag XXV was the 119 Air Defence Battery from CFB Chatham, New Brunswick, scoring several kills over the CLAWR.

A Canadair CC-144 Challenger belonging to 412 Sqn. from CFB Ottawa, Ont. departs Cold Lake after dropping off dignitaries to observe Maple Flag Operations.

CC-130E Hercules' from CFB Trenton and CFB Namao made several tactical drops over the range at Maple Flag. Canadian and American Hercules' flew out of CFB Namao due to the lack of ramp space available at Cold Lake. Hercules' were escorted by CF-18's F-16's and F-15's over the range to make their drop and get out.

A Canadian Hercules breaks to elude its attackers. When need be the Hercules can "yank and bank" down in the weeds to evade an attack.

American C-130's also played a significant role at Maple Flag. Canadian and American Hercules' flew similar missions. This C-130E belongs to 165th TAG from Savanah, Georgia.

C-141B Starlifters also played a vital role for Maple Flag. Starlifters were constantly flying in and out of Cold Lake bringing support equipment and parts for USAF aircraft. Starlifters brought everything from APU's to trucks and threat emitters to Maple Flag.

One E-3B Sentry (75-0558) from the 552nd AE&CW from Tinker AFB was based at Cold Lake for the duration of Maple Flag. The Sentry would launch in the morning and not recover until late afternoon when the afternoon launch had recovered for the day. The 552nd would direct the air battle over the skies of Cold Lake and insure that safety was adhered to on the range, especially in the case of a mid-air.

Three UN-1N Twin Huey's from the 40th ARRS served along side Canadian CH-118's for Search and Rescue during Maple Flag and to also ferry personnel and equipment back and forth on the range.

Six A-7D Corsair's from the 138th TFS, Tulsa ANG, came to Maple Flag. This will probably be the last visit for the "SLUF" at Maple Flag. Most A-7 units will convert to the F-16 within the next two years. (Photo by Pete Wilson via Author)

A mixed bag of aircraft. An A-7 of the 138th TFG taxis by F-15E's of the 4th and a CF-18A of 410 Sqn.

A CF-18A folds his wings and heads back to the apron after another successful mission.

Carrying a Philips Matra Phimat chaff dispenser still painted in the desert pink on the outboard pylon, FlLt. Sampson taxis Jaguar (XX962) for an afternoon hop. This aircraft belongs to No. 6 Sqn., the "Flying Can Openers".

What is left of the "Spitfire" painted on XX733. No.6 Sqn is still operating eight aircraft in the Persian Gulf area out of Incerlik, Turkey.

The RAF sent nine GR. MK. 1A Jaguars from RAF Coltishall. Each of the three squadrons, No.6, 41 and 54 were represented with three aircraft each. Each squadron rotated personnel through every two weeks to participate in Maple Flag. This Jaguar belongs to No. 54 Sqn.

With the canopy cracked to cool off the pilot, a Jaguar of 41 Sqn. taxis back to his parking spot. More than once RAF pilots claimed kills on F-111's, F-15's and F-16's during Maple Flag.

Jaguar XZ360 settles down at the end of runway 30R after a low level sortie. The aircraft is carrying a 1200 liter fuel tank on the center line station along with a chaff dispenser.

Jaguars return from an afternoon sortie. This picture can also make the reader appreciate the ruggedness of the Jaguar.

S/L Graham Wright was head of air operations for the RAF during period one for Maple Flag XXV. Although he is in front of a No. 54 Sqn. Jaguar he belongs to No. 6 Sqn.

No. 6 Sqn., "Flying Can Openers" prepares to taxi to the active. This Jaguar is in the colours of 54 Sqn. but is flown by No. 6 Sqn. aircrew for period one.

A crew chief makes any final checks over his aircraft before the pilot arrives. On the outer starboard station is a Phimat chaff dispenser with two 1000lb. bombs on the two inner station and a ALQ-101 jamming pod in outer port station.

A close-up view of the Phimat chaff dispenser.

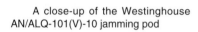

A close-up of the Westinghouse AN/ALQ-101(V)-10 jamming pod

Four Jaguars return from their morning strike against the Fantasians. Four Jaguars will follow behind. The lead Jaguar is about to do a break over the field.

No.6 Sqn. pilots return for a de-brief back in their trailer before attending a package de-brief at Maple Flag HQ.

A mixed bag of Jaguar's on the ramp. As you can see by the picture, Jaguars have a small problem with leaking, hence the oil drums.

Two Jaguars reach for the sky at the 2,000ft mark on 30R. The Jaguar needs allot of runway to takeoff when carrying any ordinance.

Four Jaguar's hold at the end of 30R for their time of departure. Four more Jaguar's will follow behind.

Jaguar, XZ360, of No. 41 Sqn. returns to the apron with the canopy open to keep the pilot somewhat cool. The temperatures are a far cry at Cold Lake than they were in Kuwait when No. 6 Sqn. was flying bombing missions.

A close-up of the front half of a 54 Sqn. Jaguar. This photo can give you an idea of how rugged looking the Jaguar really is marking it an excellent platform for its mission, air-to-ground.

No. 216 Sqn. from Briz Norton was responsible for ferrying crew and supplies between the U.K. and Canada. Once every two weeks a KC MK 1 Tristar would perform the long journey between the two countries.

1/144 AIR SUPERIORITY SERIES

4550 F-117A NIGHTHAWK '37th TFW

4522 CF-18A HORNET
'410 COUGAR SQUADRON'

4534 F-15E DUAL-ROLE FIGHTER
'336th TFS, 4th TFW'

4535 F-16C NIGHT FALCON
'421st TFS, 388th TFW'

4552 F-14A WOLF PACK CAG
'VF-1'

DS-3 TORNADO GR.1 RAF NO.15
SQUADRON 'MIG EATER'

DS-6 A-6E INTRUDER
VMA-533 'HAWK'

4549 A-10A DESERT HOG '917th TFW'

"STEPS AHEAD
.........ALWAYS"

PLASTIC MODEL KITS

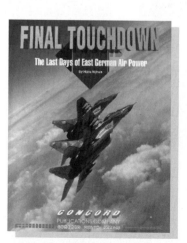